STORIES FROM THE

EGYPTIAN DESERT

Stories from the Egyptian Desert

by His Grace Bishop Macarius

ST SHENOUDA MONASTERY
SYDNEY, AUSTRALIA
2010

STORIES FROM THE EGYPTIAN DESERT

COPYRIGHT © 2010
St. Shenouda Monastery

First published in Arabic by: El Baramouse Monastery, 2003.
Translated to English by: Magdy Fahim
Illustrations by: Emad Attia.

———————

ST SHENOUDA MONASTERY
8419 Putty Rd, Putty, NSW 2330
Sydney, Australia

www.stshenoudamonastery.org.au

ISBN 13: 978-0-9805171-5-6

Cover Design: Shenouda Andrawis

CONTENTS

PREFACE

These stories were first published in Arabic between 1988 and 2002. They were printed many times, either separate or together in one book. The readers' enthusiasm to this series showed the big need for this kind of writings.

Some of the stories are true, they did happen. Others are true in part. The rest are fiction. Each story contains a certain idea to deliver a spiritual lesson. This is done in the form of a story, to make it as enjoyable as possible.

This is an opportunity for the reader who could not visit the monasteries to learn about the monastic life, the struggle of the fathers and the wars of the devil. In these short stories we tried to convey some of the fathers' philosophy in asceticism, dying to the world and how they rejected the pleasures of life to be filled from Christ and ultimately unite with Him.

I wish that God may work in the heart of the reader in the coming pages, through the prayers of H.H. Pope Shenouda the third and his partner in the apostolic ministry H.G. Bishop Isidoros, Bishop of Al-Baramoos monastery in Shehit wilderness. I would also like to thank Bishop Arsanious who revised this book.

Glory be to God forever, amen.

HE TOOK OFF

Father Serapion went out to the wilderness to pass some time at sunset. This was his daily habit.

He used to spend his time walking on the sand, or sitting down, playing with pebbles or caught up in meditation. He stood up to praise the Lord, chanting what he knew of hymns and songs. He used to pray very powerful prayers. Sometimes he experienced what the skillful fathers call "ecstasy", or "caught up."[1]

---

1   It is a state of amazement and ecstasy. This is what St. Paul experienced, when he said, "... was caught up to the third heaven--whether in the body or out of the body I do not know, God knows." (2 Cor 12:2). Also St

Father Serapion was a very simple man in his dealings with his brothers in the monastic communion. He never argued or grudged. He had no special desires in the monastery. His cell was no different to that of a new brother[1] waiting for the recommendation of the monastery to become a monk.

Although he loved everyone, he had no closeness with anyone. If someone praised him, his face would turn red with shyness and he would make no comment. If someone mistreated him unintentionally, or even intentionally, he felt the insult was directed to someone else.

He led his life enjoying peace of mind and stability of thoughts. Everyone was holy and pure in his eyes. He felt he was the only one who needed to acquire the purity of heart and the flowing love.

In addition to his great reverence in church, he never noticed who was praying, or whether the prayer took a long time. At communion time, he entered the sanctuary quietly with his shining face and slight bow that the fathers of the monastery got accustomed to. When he walked, he seemed to suffer from a little lameness in his left leg. He bowed to every monk he met, with his hand to his chest, saying, "Peace to you, father".

As for his chaste body, it never complained of his ragged clothes or his old scarf, which had become an off-green colour with age.

John when he said, "I was in the Spirit" (Rev 1:10)

1   A person seeking monasticism is called "a Brother" or "a Novice." He wears a blue or white tunic. When he is ordained a monk, he is called "a father". He wears black.

He loved his cell very much. He felt it was his mother, throwing himself into her arms. It maintained his secrets. He regarded it as a spiritual lab, a place that contained all his spiritual experiences, echoed with all his sighs and strong self-reproach. This cell witnessed the light emitting from his hands and the many angels and saints who visited him.

He had a big stone in the corner of his cell. He used to sit on it with a very old plate containing olive seeds in front of him. He smoothed them, one by one, from all sides and then made a hole in the middle. After this, he inserted a string in the hole. When done, he would have a rosary that he gave to another monk as a gift.

He had very pleasant ways of offering those presents. Beside the old well in the monastery, he met Brother Joseph. He asked him in his usual gentle manner, "Have you got a rosary?" Joseph answered him hesitantly, "No, my father, do you need one?" Father Serapion said, "No, but I have one that I don't need, here it is. It is for you. I am sure you will pray for me whenever your holy fingers handle its rough beads".

He might also leave the rosary hanging from a door handle, together with a small piece of paper on which he wrote, "This rosary belongs to Father (...)." He feared that the person receiving the gift would leave it, thinking it was not his.

If you tried to examine Father Serapion's thoughts, you would find that he had a peculiar principle. He was an expert in defending others and finding excuses for them.

He considered that the ordinary level was to forgive others for mistreating us, but the spiritual level would qualify us to find excuses for them. In defending others he never lied, exaggerated, or sought far-fetched probabilities, but he sought the good aspects in the character of the accused person and focused on them. He mentioned numerous probabilities to justify what he had committed. In all that, he never hesitated to learn from the mistakes of others. As for his administration in peace, he never participated in a dispute, or caused pain to others.

Someone narrated a funny story about him. Once a little mouse managed to get into his cell. He saw it, but did not try to drive it out. The mouse liked its life there, feeding on the monk's food and sharing his place, running here and there in pleasure. The mouse grew and began to harm the father. Father Boktor advised him to kill the mouse, or at least drive it out of the cell, but he protested, saying, "Why should I do wrong to it, whereas its life and mine are in the hands of God?"[1]

In general, Father Serapion acted like a stranger in everything. The fathers loved him very much. Most of them considered him their ideal, and tried to consult him whenever they faced an unusual situation. However, the blessed father often resorted to silence and excused himself.

Satan moved some negligent brothers to spread a rumor that Father Serapion had a mental disorder. This

---

[1] The main purpose of mentioning this incident is to highlight the virtue of peace in this father's life. In fact, getting rid of insects and rodents, especially those that carry diseases and impact cleanliness of a place, does not go against a person's gentleness. It is not a sin to be condemned for.

happened as a result of what seemed to beginners as strange behaviour. For example while he is speaking he would stopped all of a sudden, stare upwards, with his mouth open, for minutes and sometimes more than an hour. Then he apologise, wipes some tears from his red beard and says that he became distracted over something. Other times he blamed his health problems for what had happened.

These rumors were done with God's permission, to protect Father Serapion from the enemy's right-handside blows[1]. They created balance between the spiritual gifts he enjoyed and the humiliation he faced. He wanted to save him from the vainglory.

The experienced fathers in the monastery realized what that distraction really was, and justified it correctly, but kept the matter secret among them. It is wise to make such matters private, for the father's sake. It is said that virtues are lost if they become well known. They also agreed upon withdrawing and leaving him alone whenever he was caught up like this.

+ + +

It is now Baounah 13th, 1462 AM (according to the Coptic Calendar).[2] All the monks decided to leave Father Serapion alone except for Brother Theodore, who was from

---

[1]   The fathers call the wars from the devil tempting him to fall into pride because of his virtues: "Right-hand-side wars". On the other hand, wars trying to stop one from doing virtues or getting him to fall into sins are called: "Left-hand side wars."

[2]   The Coptic (Egyptian) calendar preceeded the church by thousands of years. It is also called the "Calendar of the Martyrs" as its first year was reset to the era of martyrdom.

Nubia. He went out from his cell around midnight to have a walk. When he passed Father Serapion's cell, he saw faint rays of light coming through the cracks between the wooden boards of the door. He found Father Serapion getting up, folding the worn out mat he slept on. In the faint light of the oil lamp, the mat appeared in a dilapidated condition, with strings hanging from it and straw scattered around it.

After Father Serapion had folded the mat and put it away, he began to talk to himself in an inaudible voice. Then he became involved in a dialogue. Theodore did not see the other person but he listened carefully trying to make out what was said. With great difficulty he was able to distinguish some individual words such as: "sunset..." "water..." "may Christ have mercy on me..." "no, no... everybody here is better than me...." Then Father Serapion's face shined. Brother Theodore was terrified by this sight and hurried back to his cell crying and beating his chest.

The next morning, he met Father Serapion at the well. As usual, he was smiling. Father Serapion bowed his head, putting his hand to his chest and greeted him kindly, "Peace to you, Brother Theodore". Brother Theodore kept watching Father Serapion. Each time he blamed himself for not becoming a monk yet....

In the next year, on the 21st of Bashans 1463, Father Serapion rose unusually early, before the bell rang to announce the beginning of Midnight Psalmody. He was accustomed to getting up early since he came to the monastery twelve years before, when he was twenty-six years old.

He left his cell and went to the cemetery of the

monastery, where he said a short prayer. Then he walked quietly to the monastery's kinopion[1], and came out with a few loaves of bread, which he put into his pocket. It was customary, at that time, to leave the kinopion open for the fathers to take what they needed. Father Serapion went back to his cell, not aware of the brother following him cautiously, at a distance.

The brother's love for the father and his pursuit of spiritual benefit drove him to follow the father to his cell. There he witnessed a 'holy hole' through which he beheld an ambassador of Heaven. He felt that the world did not deserve his footsteps. He found him counting on his fingers, mentioning the fathers in the monastery: Father Severus, Father Personophius, Father Shenouda, Father Dometianos, brother... etc.

Father Serapion was ready to leave the cell. Brother Theodore hastened to hide; for fear that Father Serapion might see him and grieve because his secret was revealed.

When he had walked away a little, he squatted at the end of the old cells building, close to the monastery walls at the north gate. He watched the fathers walking like ghosts in the dark, on their way to church. The bell had rung for the midnight prayer. When he was sure that all the monks had left their cells, he sneaked to the corridor and kissed the cell doors in eagerness and pleasure, murmuring in a low voice. Theodore could not make out what he was saying.

---

[1] Kinopion" is a Greek word which means the "Life of communion." Later it was used to name the area in the monastery that contained the bakery, kitchen, dinning room (table) and Bethlehem (Room where the offering Bread is prepared).

Then he entered the church. On meeting each monk he held the monk's hand in both hands and kissed it with joy mixed with reverence. During the Holy Liturgy he seemed as if he was hiding something. He stood leaning against the wall, sometimes rubbing his eyes or scratching his beard. Brother Theodore kept following him.

The Holy Liturgy was finished and everyone was released. Father Serapion did not go to his cell as the other fathers did. He sat on the fence of the small garden at the centre of the Monastery. After a while, he began to move around among its seven palm trees, feeling them. He made sure not to tread on the beans and vegetables planted there. He then went back and sat on the fence, to draw lines in the earth with a branch that he found beside him.

On the fence he seemed a bit worried. He sometimes rubbed his hands together and then rubbed them against the fence. Finally, he rose quietly, dragging his feet, and left the place.

Here Brother Theodore stopped   following him. He had to go to his work in the kinopion, helping Father Theophan.

+ + +

That day was the feast of Abba Arsanious, the tutor of the king's sons. After the Vesper prayers, the monks went out of the church, as usual, heading for the southern gate of the monastery to go out into the wilderness on a spiritual retreat. Each time, they went in a different direction. In a few minutes, they were scattered away from the monastery.

Father Serapion went east side. He walked further than everyone. Father Theopetras was the last to see him walking in determination, with the wind resisting his shabby clothes and worn out shawl, making an audible hissing.

When darkness fell, the fathers started making their way back to the monastery gate. Father Serapion did not come back. The fathers were not aware of that until noon the following day, when Brother Theodore spread the strange news, in surprise and anxiety. He went that night, according to his habit, to the cell of the blessed father. He wanted to get his daily enjoyment through the hole in the door, but he didn't find the father in his cell. He stayed there till the morning, but still Father Serapion didn't come back. Brother Theodore waited till noon, and couldn't wait any longer. He announced what he had found out to everyone.

In a commanding tone, but with proper monastic politeness, Father Shishoy assigned seven monks to search for Father Serapion. He said to them bitterly, "Let's pray that he is safe from any wild animal and that no trouble may have occurred to him." The fathers responded, muttering with bowed heads.

At sunset, the Abbot gave instructions to ring the bell continuously. The fathers took turns to ring it throughout the night, hoping that Father Serapion would find his way to the monastery guided by the sound.

The elder Father Yousab sat by the monastery's gate. He implored Brother Philemon to take him there, as he was blind. He tried to follow up what was happening and know the results of the search.

The search squad has not returned yet. The strong winds in the open desert made their mission more difficult. They began to return to the monastery around 10 pm, with bowed heads. The Abbot looked at them and understood what had happened.

The search went on for a whole month in vain. Gloom was apparent on all faces in the monastery. Prayers were raised and fasting was observed for the father's sake, but Serapion did not come back.

The Abbot asked Father Serapion's father of confession, confidentially, if he knew a reason for what had happened. The latter apologised gently saying, "All I know is that he was caught up many times. Every time he told me, except this time."

Long years elapsed, following this incident, without any satisfactory explanation. Father Serapion appeared three times in visions, once to the Abbot, a second time to Father Theophan, and a third time to Brother Theodore (who is now a monk named Bebnoudah).

The three of them saw Father Serapion with the same shining face, red beard, and slight bow with his head. But no one could remember what he told him exactly, or the conversation that took place between them. They agreed upon one thing; they had a strong feeling that Father Serapion was still alive.

The story of Father Serapion was passed on from generation to generation. The elders narrated it to the new brothers, pointing their fingers at Father Serapion's cell and in particular to the statement inscribed on the wall "Father Serapion went out and never came back".

As time passed, the story became almost like a legend. The new generations could not easily believe that such a story could have happened. Maybe it is the lack of faith, or probably the incident was too old.

+ + +

We are now at the beginning of the month of Mesra.... Father Serapion woke up by a sound like the howling of a wolf. He sighed in relief and thought of going back to the monastery before the door was closed.

Approaching the monastery he noticed, from a distance of that the monastery had changed in appearance. The big building on the north side was not there any more. It was there two hours ago, when he went out for his walk.

And what is that new wall... and that....

When he reached the gate, he rang the doorbell, with shaking hands. His heartbeats raced ahead of the bell.

The doorkeeper monk said, "Who's there?"
"I'm Serapion, Father Elijah. Please open the door."

He heard some screeching sound behind the door and the door opened, but he did not find Father Elijah. He saw a monk he didn't recognise.

Father Selwanis, the doorkeeper, greeted him but he did not respond. He was totally confused. Father Selwanis could easily see it in his eyes. He said to him, "Come in, Father. Is it your first time to visit our monastery?" Father Serapion was still amazed at what he was seeing....

Where is the guesthouse? Where has the old block of cells gone? What was that tall building in front of him? Where is...? What is this...? The doorkeeper monk tried, in vain, to draw the visitor's attention. Father Serapion was about to scream, out of surprise. The Fathers gathered to welcome him and thank him for visiting their humble monastery.

He cried out, "I'm Serapion. I went out only two hours ago. Now I can't find the monastery or my brothers." He began to cry. The fathers tried to comfort him. They were confused themselves, looking at him in astonishment. This did not last long. God inspired a holy monk, who took the visiting father's hand, and they went up to the monastery's old library. He asked him, "Could you please look up your name in this huge register". Father Serapion agreed.

They went through the pages one by one, without finding his name, up to one hundred and fifty years ago. The job needed more patience. The monk turned over pages... until Father Serapion leapt from his place, his finger almost piercing the register, pointing at his name on a line: "Here it is!"

> Girgis Henein Abdel Messeih
> Date of monasticism: 1451 (Coptic Calendar)
> Monk new name: Serapion
> Town: Memphis

In the column for date of death, the following was written, "He went out and did not come back". Only this statement was written next to his name.

He looked at the calendar hung on the library wall. It was the Coptic year 1619. They agreed to keep this matter a secret. However, light cannot be hidden. The secret was well known in less than a month... but God took Father Serapion to His eternal rest.

Where was he? What did he do? How did he live all those years... and many other questions. No one could answer them. Father Serapion remains a mystery to be solved in God's heavenly glory.

AT SUNSET

It was this part of the day when darkness covers every inch in the monastery except for faint lights coming under the door of the cells. At that time, the electricity was not yet connected to the monastery and they depended on a gasoline generator to light the early part of their nights. Every now and then, you could hear a soft voice raising prayers, reading the Bible or singing a nice praise to God. This is the custom every night. The monastery never finished praises or prayers.

It was just after midnight. The doorkeeper - I mean

the monk responsible for the monastery's gate was already asleep. Why should we judge him? He did not get enough sleep for the past two days.

The gate bell rang three times, ordering him to get up. After a few silent moments, it rang three more times. Father Sheramon paid attention to the sound but continued in his sleep thinking it was a dream. A voice came, "Father Sheramon... Father Sheramon."

The doorkeeper woke up; the voice seemed to be in a hurry. He jumped from his sleep, made the sign of the cross, saying to himself, "I hope everything is good, please God give me wisdom." When he reached the gate, he asked who it was and the answer came, "I am Oranious."

Now, Father Sheramon wasn't worried anymore. Comfort came to his heart and he opened the gate's bolt. As for Father Oranious, he was a sixty-four year old monk. He lived in solitude in a cave near the monastery. He used to come to the monastery every now and then carrying important news or an eerie warning. The fathers looked upon him with mixed feelings of honor and fear. They had all become used to his surprises.

Father Sheramon greeted him saying, "What is happening Father Oranious?" He answered, "No, I am not coming in; I am in a hurry. I have to go back to my cave. Please tell Father Bishoy that he is going to depart to heaven tomorrow after sunset. Please ask him to pray for me when he reaches the glory." He excused himself, going back, like a soldier who has delivered an import message in war.

Father Sheramon was surprised. Tears came down in his eyes. He did not know whether he was crying because he is going to miss his brother or he was sad that he was not ready yet for joining his brothers who departed before him. He dried his tears, checked his head-cover and went directly to Father Bishoy's cell. He was relieved to see light coming under his door. He stood for a couple of seconds until he got the courage to order his fingers to knock on the door.

The soft voice coming from inside ceased. Father Bishoy opened the door, pretending that he was asleep. They greeted each other. Father Sheramon leaned on Father Bishoy and whispered, "Be happy, I have good news for you. Today you will depart to the wedding and you will be clothed with glory. The blessed Father Oranious brought me the news a few minutes ago. He came especially from his cave to tell you that you are leaving today, after sunset."

He did not wait for an answer, but added, "I will leave you now and we will meet after the Divine Liturgy to pray together so that your joy is complete."

+ + +

"Bishoy...Bishoy.... It is time to leave. Be joyful, o my soul and be happy, O my heart."

The first thing he thought about was to continue with his prayer, "I thank you God with all that is within me. My senses thank You on my behalf for You have called me on this blessed morning to be raised by Your side. Blessed is that day. Blessed is Your coming to me and my going to You. I was searching for You in many places and today I will be in You. Nothing can move me away. As for my body that you entrusted with my spirit, which is your breath, I hope it is perfect before You without any corruption or defilement of the world.

Today I give you back your gift. Starting today, there is no illness, no sadness of heart, no lusts, no devil... no anger within me. I feel that all the years of my life have passed as few moments. Thanks You, O the Spirit of God, the all-holy. Rejoice all that is within me with the Lord. The Saviour of my soul has crowned me with victory. How much I missed you, Father Anthony. How much I missed you, Father Moses ...all of you, the cloud of witnesses."

He decided to clean out his cell. He then remembered that he only left the mat he slept on and the blanket he used as a cover. He also had a bible and six spiritual books. As for his dish, he used to leave it outside his door. This was his custom since he came to the monastery.

He started walking across his narrow cell. He was so happy that he wanted to dance. He thought about visiting the fathers to receive their blessing but he changed his mind since it was late. It was inappropriate to visit someone at that time of the night. He went out instead to visit the monastery's cemetery. When he reached it, he started kissing its walls. Tears came to his eyes. These were the tears of happiness. Very soon he too would be released. He had lived all his life waiting for this moment. He remembered the saying of St. Isaac, the Syrian: "The traveling merchant is watching for the land and the monk is looking up for the hour of death." He remembered Father Shishay, a monk who departed five months ago. He whispered, "I am coming to you Father Shishay."

He left the cemetery and went to the church. He could not stop himself from singing. He started to chant the hymn of the Resurrection (Khristos Anesti). [1]

The midnight praises bell rang. He imagined himself ringing the bell at the gate of paradise and the angel opening for him and leading him inside with the victorious.

The fathers started coming to church. Father Bishoy stared at each one of them, bidding them farewell. He stood quietly, praising with them. He also noticed Father Sheramon standing by his side.

When the liturgy was over, everyone in church knew the news that it is Father Bishoy's time to depart. They followed him to his cell.

---

1   Khrictoc Anecti is a Greek hymn that is chanted during the liturgy in the Feast of Resurrection and the following fifty days.

This was the last time that they would be able to talk with him and listen to him. Their eyes were filled with light from his angelic face. Bishoy's face was full of happiness. He felt great comfort in his whole body. Although he was known to be of little talk, he talked a lot that day. He included a request to them that they pray for him that God may accept him, forgiving his mistakes and sins.

One of the fathers asked him for a word of benefit. He said, "Yes. I will not deny it since I am going to my desire. I lived my whole life knowing that Christ is waiting for me in heaven. He will be joyful with me and I with Him. He will reward me for any troubles in my sojourn time on earth. I told myself, 'It is a waste to occupy myself with anything else around me while the Lord Christ is watching me from His heaven with love and longing. Whenever I stood up to pray, I would tell Him, 'Yes, My Lord. I have the same longing and the same eagerness. But let it be Your will not mine.'

As for my falls and my sins, I had great hope in my heart that would fix all what is ruined without wasting any time in sorrow or despair."

+ + +

It was approaching three p.m. One of the fathers could not hold his tears. Two more fathers joined him. There was a moment of silence before Father Policarp invited everyone to pray together. They praised as never before and prayed with one heart. Everyone was hoping for the time he will join Father Bishoy.

When they were done, Father Jeremiah asked the fathers to leave. He stayed with Father Bishoy to receive his last confession. He prayed the absolution for him and then left.

Horrible sounds were heard from Father Bishoy's cell in the distance. It seemed the devil was trying to ruin his joy after he had escaped him.

When the fathers finished the Vespers prayer, they went to Father Bishoy's cell to find that he had departed already. He was lying, facing east, with his hands on his chest, making the sign of the Cross.

A white dove was seen flying over the monastery for a few hours above the place where Father Bishoy stayed. It was a remarkable day... joy... a chance for meditation... a check with one's soul.

This incident occurred at the beginning of the previous century with one of the blessed fathers who lived in our monastery. I narrated it in a form of the story.

THE SPRING OF WATER

It was Saturday evening. A monk went to prepare for baking the Offering Bread (the Qorban) for the liturgy the next morning. He used to knead the dough at night, adding a little yeast and then baking it later during the Midnight Psalmody.

When the monk went to Bethlehem[1], he found that the water jar located just outside the door was spilled on the ground. Knowing that this must have been done by someone intentionally, the kind monk sighed and said in a low voice,

1   This is the name for the place where Offering Bread is baked, in similarity to where Our Lord was born.

as if talking to himself, "May God defeat you, Satan. You want to delay holding the Liturgy service in the morning. But no! With Christ's grace this would not happen, even if I had to bring the water myself from the spring it wouldn't be a problem." He then said, "O God, defeat Satan's counsel and give us power over him."

There were only nine monks in the monastery at that time. They used to bring water from a spring several hundred feet away from the monastery, and they also brought firewood from the mountain. For both errands, they used a quiet and obedient donkey that they have had for several years. It was assigned a suitable room to stay in the monastery. The monks were very kind to it, never overburdened it, and were generous with food and water. They often had pity on it and exempted it from work, sometimes even bearing extra efforts to themselves.

The other needs of the monastery: flour, sugar, tea, legumes (usually beans and lentils), clothes, and other things were provided to the monastery through a caravan of camels once every four months. The monks had to make provisions and organize their lives till the next caravan arrived. That monk remembered that one time the caravan was delayed, so he and his brothers did not have any flour for bread. They collected whatever breadcrumbs they could find, cleaned them from dust, and soaked them in water so that they could be swallowed easily. The crumbs that remained were placed on the marble board they used for the Offering Bread. When it was time for the next meal, they soaked them in water again, and so on, until the caravan arrived and they got flour to bake and food to cook; after spending a few days living on a handful of lentils thrown into boiling water to obtain a pale yellow kind of cooked food.

Their life was hard....

An elderly monk had ridden the donkey and gone out to do some work in the mountain. As it was the only donkey in the monastery, our monk knew that he had to carry the water pots on his shoulders in order to bring the water from the spring. He made for the gate, looking out at the mountain, for the elderly monk might be coming back with the donkey and the stones he had gone out to bring.

He was surprised to see the donkey standing beside the gate, tied to a rope. He wondered how the monk had arrived without his awareness, and why he hadn't driven the donkey to its room inside, but he said to himself, "Well, I would have had to carry the water vessels on my shoulder, one after another, and walk with them full of water all this distance. Thank You God for caring for me."

He set off to bring the vessels from inside. They were made of sheet metal, each having two handles and a lid to

prevent the water being spilt during the journey, with the donkey shaking and jolting. He began to fix the saddle on the donkey's back, putting a vessel on each side.

Here he remembered how Saint Moses the Black used to carry all the fathers' vessels, one after another, to fill them with water from a spring far away from the monastery, and how Satan, the enemy of all righteousness, envied him, as Satan is 'wise in evil'.

He said once more in a low voice, "May God shame you, Satan, with all your forces and thoughts... Do you still battle people and never stop fighting the righteous who strive in the wilderness?!"

The day was about to end, and the sun was receding. He leaned on the stake, to untie the rope and pull the donkey. He thought of riding it on his way to the spring, and walking beside it on the way back, taking pity on it because of the water it was going to carry.

When he started to mount the donkey, it seemed unwilling to bear that human burden, but the monk compelled it to carry him, by jumping to its back and nudging it, in a sign that the donkey knew well, urging it to go ahead, just as the monks used to urge it, saying, "Get along, you blessed."

On his way, as usual, the father began to pray in silence. Here he recounts what happened: "After a while, as my voice began to become louder, the donkey began to bray noisily. I was surprised at that and said sarcastically, "Maybe it likes silence, or is practicing it!! Maybe it is bored of too much talking and noise and thus is keen on silence."

After arriving at the spring I dismounted, grabbed the rope, and tied it to an old tree beside the spring. I began to get water from the spring and pour it into the two vessels, one after the other, and filled them to the brim. This spring was amazing. The level of water rose in it whenever the monastery needed additional amounts of water. For example, this happened when we had visitors and when we planted a new piece of land near the spring.

I put them back into the saddle. Earlier I had collected some grass as a reward for the donkey, but I noticed it didn't touch it. I said to myself, 'Maybe the monk who had been riding the donkey was generous to it. I wanted to reward it for the extra work it was doing, but it seemed unwilling to eat.'

I set off on my way back to the monastery, walking in front of the donkey, holding the rope in my hand. I stopped at the gate. When I urged the donkey to get in, it resisted so violently that its load was about to fall down. The more I urged it, the more it refused, so I gave up, content with that achievement, which was unexpected. I tied the donkey in the same spot where I found it first.

I began to unload the two vessels, one after the other, and then carried them inside to empty them into several earthenware vessels, beside the oven. Then I put the vessels back into the saddle on the donkey's back, saying to the donkey as if it understood what I said, 'I am sorry, we will have to fill them again. I know you are exhausted, but I will reward you as soon as we are through with this task.'

The donkey just grumbled and growled.

I repeated the job. On my way I felt comfort in my heart. I forgot the donkey's love of silence and quiet and began to recite a part from the Liturgy prayers. To be honest, my voice is not mellow, sweet or comforting, but hoarse and croaked.

It was my turn to pray the Holy Liturgy service next morning, so I wanted to rehearse what I would say. In fact I tried to master the hymns through the lessons that the blind monk living with us taught me, but in spite of his patience, I did not make much progress. The problem lies in my laziness and weak aptitude.

I got enthusiastic, feeling a sudden ecstasy, and my voice grew louder. The donkey became excited and brayed in a disgusting way. I protested saying, 'I wonder at you! You get bored of prayer and praising the Lord. What did you expect then? To hear me singing?'

As soon as I said this, it seemed that the donkey approved of what I said. I continued, 'You amaze me! It seems so strange since you spent six years in the monastery. Maybe my voice is not nice? Maybe, who knows!? Don't get angry with me.'

I ignored what was happening, and told myself it was just a coincidence. How did I know it was bored with what I was saying? Therefore, I started again rehearsing a part of the commemoration of Saints in the Holy Liturgy, 'Our Father Paul of Tamoh and Ezekiel his disciple, my masters...'

I did my best to perform well, but the donkey grumbled again. When I rebuked it in the name of the Lord, it sprang high up, causing the rope to slip from my hand and the load of water vessels to be thrown off its back.

As it was about to run away, I shouted ordering it to stop. It did, unwillingly. I went forward to the donkey, put the vessels back in their place, and pulled the animal away in silence. I was burning with anger and amazement. I preferred to keep silent and stopped rebuking the animal, as it might not only run away but then I would have to carry the water on my shoulders to the monastery. I told myself that I would rehearse the prayer in my cell at night, taking my time. Therefore I settled on praying silently during the third trip. Eventually all the vessels that I wanted to fill were filled, in addition to a clay jar beside my cell, covered with sack cloth that I used to wet with water in order to get cool water.

I went out to load the donkey to its room, but it refused to get in. I pulled the rope with all my strength, but the donkey was strong and sturdy. At that moment it seemed as if it had got the strength of ten donkeys together. I held the rope with both hands and pulled strongly, but it slipped, making a noise.

I held it again and tried to use force, but the donkey stuck its forelegs into the ground, throwing its body backwards. I felt my hands numbed by the strong pressure of the rope. As soon as I tried to release the pressure and hold the rope again, it slipped from my hands. The strange donkey retreated backwards for a distance before getting away from the gate towards the desert. When I tried to chase it, it raised a dense cloud of dust and suddenly vanished.

I stood confused, not knowing what to do! It was a terrible sight, and I had never seen anything like it. I didn't know why our kind donkey had changed like that. While I was standing confused, I saw a monk coming in the distance, riding our donkey.

Just then I realized what had happened and shouted from the depth of my heart, 'May the Lord defeat you, Satan.' I think God was punishing Satan for spilling the water by getting him to help me refill it." One of the elders of that monastery told me this story. I have written it here with few modifications.

A FATHER'S SACRIFICE

The donkey looked up at Father Nopher when he entered the stable located at the western area of the monastery. It was begging him to release it from this hard and boring work that lasted for years.

But the monk was obliged, because this is the arrangement of the abbot. It is the need of the monastery. The fathers discovered a method for preparing a material to be used in the building work around the monastery. They used to collect gypsum from the desert, burn it in an oven and then grind it in a special mill.

The monk entered into the stable to release the donkey.

He tapped on its back saying, "Come on, you blessed one." If the donkey was given a choice, it would have chosen to be locked in the stable forever from this work. It wished that all the days of the week were Sundays so that it could be relieved from this work.

In the grinding room, the monk tied the donkey to the yoke. He put a cover on its eyes and gave it a small push on its back as a signal to start work. The donkey started moving slowly, turning a wooden bar, fixed to a pole in the middle. The pole carried a big stone to grind the gypsum.

Time passed by very slowly. The donkey turned in circles, grinding the small pieces of gypsum. A huge amount of white particles filled the air to cover the monk's clothes and enter his lungs. The monk stood there, watching the donkey working. He rearranged the stones into one line under the big stone every now and then, while praying some small prayers.

Whenever an amount of gypsum is ground, he packed it in preparation for the builders to pick them up.

As days passed by boredom started to sneak to the heart of the monk. He sat one night, talking to himself, "What is the need for all that? They say the goal of the work is to gain the virtues but the exhaustion prevents me from finishing my spiritual duties. It makes me want to complain more and be less tolerant."

He felt his shoulders, the area that had dead skin as a reason of carrying the baskets of gypsum to and from the mill. He spent more than four years in this mill. And his clothes needed to be washed everyday. And the coughing that he was suffering from because of the gypsum particles.

He wandered with his mind. Still awake, he saw a dream. The mill has totally disappeared from the monastery and is replaced with nice and healthy cell where he is reading and praying and chanting nice hymns.

He got an idea. Why doesn't he go to the abbot and asks that he is relieved from the work in the mill. He quickly smiled. How can he do this? What reasons will he provide to the abbot to convince him?

He returned to himself to find the donkey had stumbled in his walk. He stood up, fixed his yoke and returned back to his thoughts. "There must be a solution... an end to this."

At night he sneaked to the mill (where the devil was dancing). He spent a few minutes there and then returned quietly to his cell. Minutes later, spurts of fires rose and voices screamed around the monastery.

The monks woke up from their sleep or paid attention from their prayers. They rushed to the source of the sound, fire and smoke. Everyone started taking action. Some carried water in jars with different sizes and shapes. Others threw in sand using palm baskets. The elders started praying, asking for God's mercy that no one is hurt.

The fire was put out. It ate everything made of wood in the mill: bars, poles, doors, windows, shelves, the yoke and the ceiling. Some zealous faces and hands were scorched a little. The fathers looked at each other, surprised, what could have happened? They thanked God, though, it could have been worse.

In Father Yakoub's cell, Father Nopher sat down to tell him what he did. He could not stop crying but his father calmed him down. He asked him to keep silent and leave all the matter in his hands.

Father Yakoub knew that the right punishment for what he did was expulsion from the monastery. But the fatherly love filled his heart. He was scared that if his son was sent out of the monastery he would get lost and fall into despair.

He thought for a long time, then he stood up to pray. After a lengthy prayer, he kissed the icon of the Lord Christ hung at his door and went out of his cell. He knew he was going to do something.

The mill had now become a spectacle that the monks came to every now and then, to watch what happened. The walls were black and the room still smelled of smoke, as a result of the fire.

Father Zechariah the abbot, stood beside the place, resting his hands on his staff wondering. Probably the fathers in the monastery were thinking at that time to consult Father Yakoub in this matter, knowing that he possessed wisdom, experience, and a big heart.

Father Yakoub surprised all of them. He wore strange clothes and was laughing hysterically. He pointed to the mill, saying, "This is my first accomplishment. I will continue in my struggle." He started laughing again, as if he was drunk.

The fathers gathered around him. They could not speak out of surprise. They knew Father Yakoub was a wise guide. He possessed the right opinion and the just judgment in any matter they faced.

He stepped towards Father Zechariah, in fake stupidity, "It is the devil's deceit; we did not come here to grind. We forgot our goal, the virtue and the repentance. I will clean the monastery. I will force you to commit to the monastic truth."

As for Father Nopher, he sat crying in his cell and did not leave it. Nobody accused him of anything. They just asked him if he may have forgotten a lit lamp before leaving the mill and he denied it.

After many discussions and debates, the fathers in the monastery decided that the elder needed to be treated. It is not the case of a burnt mill any more. It was the problem that Father Yakoub had lost his mind as they thought.

Father Zechariah, accompanied by two monks, went to his cell. After some hesitation they told him, "You are exhausted and tired above the limit. We have seen that it is better for you to rest for a while in a quiet place and then return to the monastery."

He did not argue with them. He did not think that it would reach the point where he would be sent to the psychiatric hospital. He accepted it though.

On the gate, the fathers were standing to bid him farewell with eyes full of questions and pity. One of his sons offered to accompany him to the place they were sending him to and stay with him there. They refused and asked him instead to pray for him.

During this, Father Yakoub was whispering to himself, "The disgrace of Christ is richness, the disgrace of Christ is richness."

In the hospital, they received Father Yakoub Saleeb Al Masoudi, registered him and diagnosed his case as a sudden mental illness. They placed him in a big room with five other patients under observation.

All the reports written about him stated that he was a normal person. He did nothing to prove otherwise either. The doctor decided to keep him for some time to make sure he was well.

One of the patients with him was a French teacher. He had the habit of walking in their room diagonally, going back and forth for a long time, each day. Except for these times, he seemed a totally normal person.

Father Yakoub knew, from him, that he used to love the French literature and that a horrible accident happened to him leading to his current condition. Sometimes he would suddenly scream and then return quiet again.

Father Yakoub saw in his fellow inmates the tortured human soul. He was sure, due to his experience and age, that the mad person thinks himself the wisest person on earth and looks down to everyone else. Father Yakoub felt he was obliged to help these people. He loved them and they returned this with bigger love and gratitude. They confided in him all their troubles and secrets, because he was an expert in the human soul and in the evil that tries to invade it.

He assured them that they were not normal humans. They are talented by nature, thinking thoroughly in everything. They do not let any situation pass without a comment or an interaction. The community just misunderstood them and failed to deal with them.

He became a father to them, talking to them and listening in return. His heart was big enough for all their mistakes and moodiness and sometimes harm. For example, the French teacher decided one time to teach him the French language. Father Yakoub obeyed to avoid any arguments. The teacher started and he listened to him following his advice. In a few months, the father was quite advanced in this new language.

The patients drew nearer to him. His effect was quite obvious in their actions. He once told them what Abba Anthony said, "Time will come when everyone will go crazy and whoever is not acting similar to them will be called the crazy one. It is not important to do what pleases the people since nothing will please them. Everyone has his own mind. We should please the Holy Spirit within us. If you question the effect of the surrounding environment and what we read and hear on our consciences, I tell you, it is better to consult those who posses the wisdom and the virtues. We should also read more."

They looked at him amazed, nodding their heads for him to continue. One of the patients was extremely happy, he picked the plastic plate in front of him and poured its contents of vegetables over his head, silently.

The father continued, "We have to realize that we cannot make all the matters of life move according to our own will. We cannot correct the entire universe at once. The matter needs deep thinking. Each of us should do his part honestly. We cannot count all the people similar to us. We have to believe in the dissimilarity."

One of the patients then cried suddenly, "But we need to fight wickedness, with no rest." "Yes, Yes. But wisely, without force. Force, as you know, is a two-edged sword." Another one kicked Father Yakoub, "You are a seller of talk." He answered, "Never. I am just telling you what I learned from you."

Days passed by. An apparent improvement was seen on all patients. They were quieter and less prone to fights and troubles. Many of them were ready to leave the hospital. The hospital director was telling his fellow doctors, "He came as a patient, but we discovered he is a doctor!"

He then added, "I am sure now. He must have faked what led him to come here. I learned a lesson, I will never forget. I should not judge by appearances."

One morning, Father Zechariah, accompanied by four monks, came to the hospital. They asked about Father Yakoub. The doctor brought them the good news that they could take him with them. He sent for Father Yakoub. When he came, he surprised everyone by saying, "Here is similar to there.... Maybe here is better...."

The director wrote in his report, "I think this father faked madness. He is sane and rational. He posses a big amount of wisdom and courteousness. Generally, his presence was a blessing for the hospital and everyone in it."

The monks accompanied Father Yakoub with them. Everyone in the hospital greeted him with great honor, some with tears.

The fathers in the monastery said about him, "Christ's disciple is a blessing where he is. He is a testimony of holiness for everyone. He sanctifies any place he lived in."

The hospital director used to come, every now and then, to visit Father Yakoub. He used to kiss his hands and then sit down to listen to his words of wisdom. He once asked him, "Why did you do that?" Father Yakoub smiled and did not answer.

This is a summary of the life of the blessed Hegumen Yakoub Saleeb Al-Masoodi:

- ❖ He was born around 1859 A.D. in the village of Al-Sheikh Masood in Tahta.
- ❖ He entered the monastery in 4th of Tobah 1601 AM[1] (1884 A.D.).
- ❖ He was ordained a priest in 9th of Hatour 1604 AM (1887 A.D.).
- ❖ And a hegumen in 14th of Babah 1613 A.M. (1896 A.D.).
- ❖ He departed in 16th of Tout 1653 A.M. (26th of September 1936 A.D.).

It worthy to note that he is the brother of Hegumen Abd Al-Maseeh Al-Masoodi Al-Baramoosi, the famous teacher.

We narrated this incident in a form a story depending on the monastery's history kept in it. We also used the oral

---

1   According to the Coptic Calendar.

tradition handled by its fathers. Some of our sources sat with father Yakoub himself before his departure.

The fathers in the monastery still remember this incident with great admiration. It is an evidence of the love of the father and his sacrifice for his children. If Christ, being righteous, died for the sinful, then this father learned from his Master. He found no problem in being punished for his son. He accepted in content and happiness.

May the blessing of his prayers be with us all, amen.

AN INVITATION TO A FEAST

The old monk walked slowly through the dusty path in the monastery. He was trying to sense his way, moving his stick right and left, to make sure he wouldn't stumble or bump into a wall.

Before he moved a few steps, a young monk approached him, kissed his hand and offered to help him reach his destination. He escorted him to a near mastaba[1] and very kindly helped him to sit on it. The young monk excused himself to leave and asked for the elder's prayers. He replied with his famous saying, "May God help you to save your soul."

1　　　　outdoor stone bench

While sitting, he does not show any movement. Nothing but his voice every now and then, singing an old song or praise that he brought with him from his village or inherited from an older monk. He had a very peculiar way of singing. His voice had both a sad and joyful tune at the same time. His songs were very special, he encouraged and rebuked at the same time.

Everyone who hears him feel that the sound is coming from eternity. He feels that he is singing up there in heaven and the voice is reaching them from there.

As time passes by, he does not know the hour. He does not differentiate between days and nights. When the monastery bell rings, they escort him to the church. When the eating bell rings, they take him there. He does not ask, what is the time. He does not know places in the monastery without being escorted there.

He is carried on the care of God and His protection. After a long time, sitting on the mastaba, he starts the journey back to his cell with the same slowness. Another monk sees him and offers to help him.

When it is sleep time, a young monk appointed by the monastery to serve him, opens the elder's cell quietly and checks that everything is ok. He asks for his blessings and prayer, goes out and locks the door from outside.

When it is time for the midnight prayers bell, the monk comes back to the elder's cell to escort him to the church. He put his hands in the elder's and accompanies him in silence to the church. The elder in all this is totally calm and safe, he does not ask nor question. He knows that they are carrying his needs when their time comes. He is sure that he is into the hands of his brothers, which are supported with God's entrusted hands.

Every meal, when the bell rings, the monk comes and escorts him to the table. He sits, eats silently and then the monk takes him to wash his hands. He gives him his tea and then takes him back to his cell or to his place on the mastaba. Also, when the time comes for his weekly bath, the same monk comes and prepares it for him and washes his clothes.

Briefly, this monk serving the elder is his eyes.

+ + +

One night, when the bell rang around 4 am, the monk went to the elder's cell. He knocked gently and entered, "Come on father, the bell rang. Let us go to the church to praise."

"What bell and which praise." The elder asked.

The monk answered patiently, "The bell for the midnight praises."

"God bless you my son. Maybe you forgot or you are dreaming."
"No, my father."

"How can it be? The bell has rung few hours back and I went to the church."

The young monk said, laughing, "What bell and which church?"

"I praised and I prayed the liturgy."

"0 my God. You must have been dreaming."

"Never, believe me. It was a nice liturgy. I believe I never felt the same comfort and peace as I felt this morning. But tell me, didn't you come and accompany me to church?"

The monk felt sorry for the elder. He thought he had some kind of sudden hallucination or he must be mixed up. He never asked about time, not even once. He usually sits for hours, not knowing how much time has passed.

The young monk tried to hold his hands to escort him to the church. He drew it away and reproached him innocently, "It was a nice liturgy. The praying father had an angelic voice. Don't you believe me? I partook from the mysteries."

The monk, who learned to be patient from the slowness of the elder, wanted to return him to his awareness. The elder put his hands in the large pocket. After a little effort, he got out a piece of the ologia[1]. He gave it to the monk who took it into his hands. He found it to be fresh. At that time of the morning, they did not start to bake the offering bread yet.

The monk was astonished. He was silent for some

---

[1] "Ologia" is a Greek word that means "nice word." It was called on the piece of the offering bread (the blessing) distributed by the priest at the end of the liturgy. They used to say a "nice word" during the distribution.

time, and then he asked the elder, "Can you please tell me what happened exactly."

"Nothing, same as I told you before. But why didn't you accompany me, maybe it was another monk. Why did you sleep until now?"

The monk did not answer. He ran to the abbot to tell him about this incident. The father knew what had happened. He took some fathers and went to the old church, under the ground. They were surprised to smell incense filling the place. The altar utensils were left without packing them and drops of water were easily seen in front of the Throne.

The fathers returned, full of happiness and comfort to the cell of the elder to explain to him what has happened. The elder received their words with extreme silence, free from any astonishment. He did not ask anything, just nodded his head.

The elder himself told me this story, ten years before his departure.

The name of the elder is: Father Andoraus Al-Samouili.[1]

---

[1] Father Andrew from St Samuel Monastery.

IT IS WAR, MONK

His name is Moses.

Moses Al-Masoodi.

Or Moses Al Baramoosi.

He loved the ascetic life since he was young. His mother told him many stories about the great monastic fathers, their struggle in the monasteries, their fight against the devils and how the angels appeared to many of them.

He loved monasticism and the monks. As soon as a monk comes to his village for some work, he sticks to him throughout the whole visit, memorizing his words, comments and actions. He kept this in his heart with pride, admiration and happiness that cannot be hidden.

He was waiting, impatiently, for the day he can leave his home and go to the monastery. Probably, he also heard about the Hegumen Abd Al-Meseeh Al-Masoodi the great, who was a monk in Al-Mohareq monastery and then moved to Al-Baramoos.

He considered every day that he was away from the monastery as a wasted day. Finally, he was able to flee the grip of his mother and sister's emotions and he departed to the valley of Sheheet, aiming at Al-Baramoos Monastery.

He started his life there, obedient in everything and to everyone. He lived, as a young monk, learning from everyone around him. He moved between different works in the monastery and gained many virtues. He became a disciple to many blessed fathers.

The main virtue that he excelled in was his great love of prayers. He would spend more time on it than anything else. He was always hungry to pray. He exceeded his monastic canon, training himself to crucify the body in his prayers. Once, he told one of the fathers that he felt the presence of Christ himself, whenever he stood up to pray.

Boredom could not catch up with him. And when it caught him, it could not overcome him. He would pray, once, kneeling on his knees, with his hands up. Another time, he prayed standing up, his hands crossed against his chest. A third time, he closed his eyes and whispered and a fourth time, chanting his prayers with a nice voice.

He used to forget everything while standing before the altar of prayers. The Divine Presence captured him until he did not feel his feet on the mat under him. If someone called him from outside, he did not hear him. Also, if anyone knocked on his door while he was praying he did not acknowledge him.

As time passed by, his face grew brighter and more angelic. His fondness in prayer increased. He was rarely seen outside his cell. When the fathers asked him to join some activity, he apologised, saying that the prayer was extremely nice and enjoyable and it was sufficient for him. He was not saying this out of pride, but innocence, as if he was talking to himself.

Many times, he was busy with prayers, while the other fathers were working. All the fathers respected his feelings and desires, but his spiritual father watched all this cautiously. Every now and then, he would warn him of the necessity of being balanced.[1]

It happened, during the midnight praises on a Sunday in Kiahk, that the father noticed that Father Moses was missing. This is unusual since the fathers used to attend the Kiahk praises and the Pascha week together, even the hermits.[2]

---

1   It is well noted that the responsibility is moved from the confessor to his father of confession if these two rules are fulfilled: - First, that the confessor confesses everything and hides nothing. - Second, to obey in everything.

But, the confession is received and cannot be extracted.

2   The hermit is a monk living a solitary life outside the monastery's walls. This can be only done after spending many years with the fathers, in the life of communion, inside the monastery.

That night, Father Mina Al-Mahalawy, the abbot, went to check up on him in his cell. He was surprised to hear strange noises coming out from his cell, something between whispering and ugliness. Instead of knocking, he listened. He was more surprised to hear some sounds similar to a snake hissing. He was disgusted and knew that this was a bad sign. He did not try to explain what he heard or analyse what was happening. He just went back to the church, absent-minded and worried. He returned again, before the end of the praises to Father Moses' cell and listened. This time, he heard his prayers as if he was singing. He was amazed and kept this in his heart.

In the morning, he met him walking slowly, according to his habit, with his worn clothes and torn shoes. He asked him, why he didn't come to church the day before to pray and praise with his brothers. He apologised, politely, that he was not feeling well. He was deprived from the blessing of his brothers. Then he said, scratching his beard, "God willing, next Saturday."

Father Mina did not comment, although the doubt was eating at him. He was worried about that father. He went to Father Simon, told him his worries and asked him to interfere to save his son.

It seemed normal that a monk prays a lot and loves the prayer, spending all his time in it. Father Moses did exactly that, forgetting his food and escaping work with his brothers. He prayed in a long way, chanting slowly, more than usual or according to their custom.

Many fathers blamed themselves, when they started comparing themselves to Father Moses.

On the other hand, those who struggled and had victory in their spiritual life, those who fought wars with the devils and Christ won on their behalf, were ignorant no more, in the tricks of the devil. They were trained in the wilderness with the skill and experience; they rang warning bells and turned on the red light.

There was a long conversation between Father Moses and his spiritual father, Hegumen Simon, "I agreed with you that you pray, matins and midnight only, then you keep your thoughts pure for the rest of the time. This is enough."

"But, I love to pray more, what is the harm in this?"

"The harm is not in prayers; it is in your disobedience."

"I broke the commandment to pray!"

"The fear is that you pray for the sake of prayers alone."

"I do not understand."

"I am afraid that the reason for your prayers is to become a praying monk who only satisfies his pride that he had reached a high level in prayers. It is well known that prayer is love, meekness and repentance."

"This is true. This is what I believe in; we have no differences."

"If this is your belief, you would not be sad and angry when I asked you to change your administration in prayer."

"What would you say, if I told you that I hear encouraging voices at some times?"

"This is blessed, but these may not necessarily be divine voices every time."

"And I also feel great comfort in prayers, especially when praying a lot."

"Maybe this is not comfort but self-satisfaction. He who does his own will gives space to the devil, the devil of the vain praise. The one who obeys his spiritual father bears great fruit, the delicious fruit of humility."

"I will try. Remember, my father, that I reluctantly obey you."

"Remember my son, that the middle way saved many."

"Forgive me and absolve me. The road is long and hard and I am not experienced."

Father Simon prayed the absolution to him and went away praying to God that He may lift up the war that the devil had declared against him. He felt that the enemy of the good has picked him when he found him a sheep that deserted the flock.

As for Moses, these thoughts started to trouble him

and the devils whispered in his ears, "Your father said that only because he is jealous of you. He didn't reach what you reached."

Moses then talked to himself, protesting, "Who said we should not pray. Instead of advancing in prayers, we retreat and decrease what we pray?"

Two years later, he moved to live in another cell, according to the order of the Abbot, so that the war may calm down. It did not. Moses did not correct his attitude; instead everyone noticed his sick solitude. He did not appear in the monastery streets any more and he was rarely seen taking some bread or beans or filling his old broken jar of water. He would walk slowly, his face full of pleasure and pride and his eyes saying to everyone, "Where are you from me, you poor one."

His father wept and went to his cell again. This time he bowed down to him and tried to kiss his feet. He asked him to leave his cell for some time and come to live with him. Moses was silent for a long time until his father calmed down a little.

Tired of keeping a big secret, he said, "You know my father; some angels came to me to bless me."

"What else, you poor one?"

"They just blessed me. They lit the space around me and encouraged me with many words."

"How many times did they come to you?"

"Eight or nine times."

"Did they tell you anything? Anything unusual?"

"No, they did not, only their appearance was delightful and their words comforting."

Father Simon sighed in sorrow, nodded down and after a period of silence, he said bitterly, "Please, if this happens again, tell me very soon."

Moses was once seen coming from Al-Hokaria[1], carrying a chicken in a bag. He entered his cell and prepared it with some vegetables. He then went out and invited some of the fathers who came and ate with him. When they finished, he prepared tea for them and talked a lot, against his custom lately.

They took the chance and tried to speak with him regarding his state and the recent jumps. He tried to avoid their questions. When he couldn't, he took permission and left the cell until everyone left.

Father Hedra, a close monk to father Moses, tried to penetrate the fence that he made around him. He asked him, "I hope you are praying for me. I need a lot of beseeching and tears these days."

"God may help us all. Believe me, there is nothing better than prayer. It is the road to God. It is the peace, the down payment to eternity."

---

[1] A village in Al-Natron Valley, near the monastery

"Yes, but I am weak. I can barely pray, completing my canon. Do you know what my spiritual father told me?"

"What did he say?"

"He said, if you are in your cell and hear some knocking, leave whatever you are doing, even prayer, and go and serve him. Then you can continue with your previous work."

"Nonsense. They just tell us this because they only care about finishing the monastery's work: building, baking, grinding, farming, receiving the visitors and other things. This is a trick from the devil to take us away from prayer."

Then he continued, waving his hands in the air, "All who are in charge do the same thing. They have the same perspective. They only talk about obedience. The theology they learn and teach is the theology of authority! Blind obedience, they want us as tools in their hands."

"Take it easy, my brother and forgive me. They work for our benefit. They know we need teaching and they are afraid from the right-hand-side wars[1]. They like things to advance little by little. They are afraid of jumps. They believe in the quality not quantity."

"Nonsense... lies and deceit. You do not know how my father is trying to chain me and hinder my advances.

---

[1] The fathers call the wars from the devil tempting him to fall into pride because of his virtues: "Right-hand-side wars". On the other hand, wars trying to stop one from doing virtues or getting him to fall into sins are called: "Left-handside wars."

He is jealous of me. Yes, mere jealousy and a heart full of hatred. It is ok, though. God has seen my patience and encouraged me."

Father Hedra knew, at that moment, that father Moses was captive to these thoughts. He tried again, "Obedience is better than sacrifice and listening is better than calves' meat. The disciple, with his obedience, becomes better than his teacher."

Moses stopped listening and refused any advice, except the one that matched his desires.

Father Hedra offered that he takes the abbot's permission for Father Moses to come to work with him in farming. Moses apologised the he cannot succeed in working with others.

Father Hedra left him, sad, asking God secretly that He may release his captured brother.

For a period after this conversation, Father Moses went out fewer times from his cell. The fathers started coming from other monasteries asking about him. Rumors spread that his hands lit and he suspended when he was praying (his legs did not touch the ground). They also said, he disappeared from his cell and from the monastery. He was an anchorite. His cell once disappeared and returned back... and....

+ + +

One night, the angels that he told his father about,

visited him. They came after the midnight prayers, round 2:30 a.m. They praised him with great talk and delivered to him the good news that heaven had recognised his works. They said, "God has ordered that you are rewarded for your struggle, weariness, watchfulness and patience, more than all the strugglers. You are going to be taken to heaven, similar to Elijah."

Then they continued in a whispering, warning voice that is full of cunningness, "But beware! Do not tell your father, he will not believe you as he did not reach your level and your holiness yet. If he heard from you what we just told you, he will prevent you. You will be denied this reward and this honor. The devil may then fight against you and throw you away from your rank. Laziness will sneak into your heart and you will lose your crown."

Moses answered quickly, "No, no... do not worry about that matter."

The angels continued, "The day after tomorrow, around midnight, at one O'clock, you should pray long as usual. Then ascend the monastery's northern wall at its east side. Wait for us, we will pick you up in a chariot to be taken to the glory. Beware, do not tell anyone, as we mentioned."

Then the angels disappeared...

The whole world shook in his eyes and the earth moved under his feet. He did not know what to do. Should he be happy? Should he cry? Is it death or really a raise to glory?

Should he tell his father or not?

But why is he puzzled and what can he tell him. His father will not understand him, he will try to hinder him.

How can he disobey a godly order? How can he be suspicious in something desired by every human?

He could not sleep that night. The next morning, he did not eat. He did not even pray. Why should he pray? Prayer is for the beginners in the spiritual path - he has arrived. God has called him in a way that never happened to anyone before. He is strong between the prophets, Elijah the Teshbite.

What an honor...

"How many times did they despise and blame me, but I endured and toiled. Finally God has crowned my struggle," he told himself.

He started tapping on the door of his cell from inside, singing,

"Fai pe pi ehooh... Fai pe pi ehooh. [1]"

He did not know that there was an evil assembly, at the same time, singing in ugly voices,

"Fai pe pi ehooh... Fai pe pi ehooh."

He was singing joyfully and unconsciously. They were singing totally conscious... in malicious joy, standing on the door of a sure victory.

+ + +

It was a special night, very cold and windy. Three monks were baking the dough for the offering bread at Bethlehem, getting ready for the liturgy.

At around 1:30 am, they heard a sound of a collision, followed by a scream out of pain. Then everything was quiet again.

The fathers jumped from their place, and went to see what happened. They ran towards the source of the sound, while making the sign of the cross and praying short quick prayers, puzzled what this may be? On their way, passing by the monastery's northern gate, they heard ugly and disgusting

---

1   Vai pe piehoou (This is the day) from psalm 117.

voices laughing. The voices decreased then started aga
until they vanished and it was all silent.

When the three fathers opened the gate, they heard
weak moaning sound. Approaching the sound, they saw
monk's body soaked in blood. They lit a match to see wh
he was.

It was Father Moses....

They quickly carried him inside the monastery. Man
monks, who were praying in their cells, had already gathere
to see what was happening.

They took him to his cell. Father Makari, who was
physician before joining the monastery, rushed to the cell t
try to help. Moving his hands, he found fractures all over hi
hands, legs and ribs and probably he had internal bleedin;
also. He plastered the broken bones and they placed him o;
a wooden sheet. Then, they gave him lemonade to drink. H
managed to take a sip with great difficulty.

All the fathers gathered around him and outside hi;
cell, wondering what happened.

Hegumen Mina, the abbot, came and asked the father;
to leave him to rest and pray for him. He then sat down
with two fathers, including father Makari, trying to comfor
him. He did not stop moaning out of severe pain.

He entered into a coma. The fathers sat around him,
surprised, full of pain and worry for Father Moses. They
raised their hearts in prayer for him. No one can answer

their question: what has really happened?

Moses woke up. Still moaning in pain, he started asking forgiveness and absolution from the fathers around him. They comforted him. He said, "I sinned. I did not submit to the warnings of my father. I fell into the deceit of the devil. They deceived me."

He tried to cry but couldn't. Father Simon came quickly, annoyed. As soon as Moses saw him, he went into a coma, again.

The next day, he was swinging between comas and waking up, spending it in pain and moaning and asking forgiveness from the fathers.

The third day, pain increased, despite the tranquilizers they gave him. It is obvious it was his last hours....

By noon, Father Moses asked the fathers to leave him alone with Father Simon. He told him what happened. Father Simon wept during the conversation, pitying his son. At the end, Father Simon prayed him the absolution, encouraged him and comforted him. They prayed together, thanking God who gave him an opportunity to offer repentance.

By sunset, all his body was swollen, his face turned black and he stopped talking. They could not move him to a hospital lest he died on the way. When father Mina felt that the end was approaching, he invited all the fathers in the monastery to be blessed from him and pray for him[1]. They gathered in his cell and they prayed the thanksgiving prayer

---

[1] This is the habit in monasteries when a monk is departing.

followed by a long litany from one of the fathers. It brought tears to their eyes. They kissed him, one after another and departed to their cells.

One and half hour later, around nine p.m. the monastery's bell rang, announcing Father Moses' departure.

+ + +

On the stairs leading to the old church in the monastery, Father Mina sat with Father Simon, listening to what happened.

Father Simon said, "They told him, the enemies of the good, 'We will come to you from above. You wait for us on the fence, near the dining table area.' In the agreed time, the poor man was waiting for them. He heard thunder noises and storms. Lightning suddenly appeared and faded. He then saw a big chariot coming, led by four horses of fire. It stopped, touching the fence and a voice came, 'Proceed, get into the chariot.'

He obeyed. He raised his right foot to get into the chariot but he was simply stepping into the air. He fell from the top of the fence, nine meters high. He slammed very hard to the ground like a big rock. He could clearly hear their laughs and mockery while he was screaming of pain."

Then father Simon continued, "Yes, he confessed everything. He revealed all his mind. Maybe the Lord did not allow that his works and struggle is wasted. He left him a chance for repentance, lest he loses his eternity..."

As for father Philemon, he was a righteous monk, whose life witnessed for his holiness. He went out one night to sit on the stone steps beside the gate of the monastery. He heard a noise. It was a group of the devils, coming to check up on the place where they had victory over Father Moses. It was even around the same time, after midnight.

Maybe Father Philemon had come to that place for that reason. As they approached, he shouted at them, in the name of the Lord, not to move. They were crucified to their places. He started praying loudly, with a pure heart and great friendship with God.

The devils screamed but he did not care. Their cries and squeals increased but he ignored them and continued praying. He asked God loudly that they would be ashamed.

They begged him to release them. He asked them, "How dare you attack God's creation, you evil ones. You know your destination is the lake of fire."

They answered him, with their ugly appearances, that they did not accomplish their task. He did not die before he repented. For that reason, they were sorry.

They promised that they would not return to that place again. He made the sign of the cross three times against them, saying, "May God disgrace you." They converted to smoke and vanished.

+ + +

This was the last scene from the life of the blessed

father, the departed Hegumen Moses Al-Masoodi AlBaramoosi. He was born in 1566 M[1], 1850 A.D. His name was Bishay Morcos. He was born in a village named, Al-Sheekh Masood in Tahta. He came to monasticism during the time of Hegumen Youhanna, the first in 1589 M, 1873 A.D. He was ordained a priest in 1594 M, 1878 A.D. during the time of Hegumen Youhanna the second. He was then ordained a hegumen in 1616 M, 1900 A.D. during the time of hegumen Mina, the first. He rested during the time of Hegumen Mina Al-Mahalawy, the abbot in 1636 M, 1920 A.D.

We narrated it, as a story with minor changes....

---

[1] This is the Coptic Calendar

AN IDEA

After spending a couple of hours thinking, absent minded, he approached his father slowly, then he begged, "Father...."

His father answered, still reading his newspaper, "Yes, dear."

The child, who hadn't reached his sixth year yet, pulled the paper from his father's hands and placed it aside. His father held him with his hands, kissed him on his forehead and said again, "Yes, dear."

"I want to become a monk".

The father answered, without paying attention, "When you grow up, you can become a monk."

"I am old enough."

"When you grow older and become a physician or an engineer then you can become a monk."

"I can grow up there."

"All the monks grew up here first then went to the monastery."

The son banged his feet to the ground, stubbornly, saying, "It is not my problem."

The father felt some seriousness in his son's desire. He liked the idea to continue this conversation, "Don't you like the idea of becoming an engineer?"

"I want to become a monk!"

"Did you see Father Takla during our visit to the monastery today?"

The son nodded his head, "Yes."

"He was a physician."

"But he makes bread in the monastery.... He gave Michael and I two loaves of bread."

"In the monastery, they do not accept the children."

"Why?"

The mother started mumbling, sitting far, following up the conversation happily. The father continued his arguments, "In the monastery, they will cut your hair."

"I will cover my head. All of them do this."

"In the monastery you cannot wear pants, shorts or colored shirts that you like."

"I will wear similar to them. They do not wear shorts."

"Mum will not be there."

The mother looked up to her son's face to see his reaction and hear his answer. The boy chose a diplomatic answer, "She will come to visit me with you."

"What about your friends in church who call you a lot and meet with you in church and school."

"I will make new friends from among the monks."

"There is no chocolate, nor cake... just beans, lentils and dry bread."

He shrug his shoulders that he does not care. The father continued, "There is also no meat."

The boy asked in sorrow, "No chicken either?"

The father was happy, thinking that finally he was able to find the obstacle that will defeat his son and finish this conversation. He added, "Of course, no chicken. You like chicken, don't you."

The boy's answer was like a slap on his face, "I do not like chicken. I want to become a monk."

The father started the struggle again, "Does the teacher beat you at school?"

"No."

"Does any one steal your sandwiches?"

"No."

"Have your mother and I bothered you."

His mother called him before he answered this question. She wanted to tempt him with a gift she had bought for him. He did not respond but started banging his feet on the ground, about to start crying, "I want to become a monk."

The father whispered to the mother, "Who knows?"

He then told his son, "Ok, we will take you to the monastery and ask the permission of the abbot there."

The boy answered quickly with his eyes sparkling with the glory of victory, "He agreed. I asked him and he agreed."

"But he did not tell me."

"He said, 'We will name you Abanoob.' He gave me his picture. I love Saint Abanoob."

His mother stood up calmly and took him to his room. He tried to escape using his small body and he succeeded returning back to his father. The father could not but continue the same conversation with him, "Aren't you afraid to stay alone in the monastery."

He knocked his fist on his father's knee answering in persistence, "No."

"So, what do you like your mother and I to bring you when we come to visit you."

He stared to the ceiling, thought a little, and then said, "Nothing."

The mother turned her face away to wipe a tear that slipped out without the son noticing it. She could not bear it any more, she told him, "Would you come with me tomorrow. I am going to the monastery."

The boy was extremely happy, his face turned more angelic with his big smile. His mother was able finally to take him to his bed. She covered him, saying, "You have to take some rest now to get up early in the morning."

He fell asleep very quickly and his childish dreams added more innocence to his face.

In the morning he was having the regular argument with his mother on what sandwiches he is taking with him to school.

Today he is a physician, married with three children. He works in an African country. I think it is Cameroon.

A GREATER LOVE

Have you heard about Michael?

Then you don't know of Monk Evlogious.

It's ok; I mean to tell you what happened to him.

While he was making his own plans, God was working secretly to secure his future and fulfill His will in him.

Michael was a student in Medical School. Marian was going to the same school, even attending the same classes.

Michael's heart was attached to her. Many times he wished the day would come when they would get married and she could share his life. In their home, Christ would come, fill their hearts and bless their thoughts. They would raise their children as an acceptable gift. Through one body, they could reach together one mind and one heart, fulfilling one goal. This was their love to Christ. He dreamt about that day, barely able to wait for it to come.

At the same time, Marian was visiting a monastery for nuns in Old Cairo. She used to spend her vacations there in spiritual retreats. She sat with the mothers, telling them about the stumbling blocks she faced in her school and the absence of Christ from some students.

She wished for a life of solitude. She waited for the day when she could lock herself up in a small and simple cell. How this cell would be nicer and bigger than the most luxurious house that a man can offer her.

She will watch in her cell until the time for the midnight praises. She will rarely go out from her cell... reading, praying, meditating and studying. She waited for that day, but her studies and her family did not give her much of a chance for all of that now.

Every now and then, Marian told herself, 'When this day comes, I will leave for the monastery without coming back. I will stay there to enjoy the spiritual comfort and drink from the spring of wisdom and virtue. I will leave the world to those who can live in it."

Michael could not tell Marian how he felt towards her,

before he finished school. When the day came when both of them finished the final year, he was encouraged to tell her about his desire to marry her. She was happy and her shyness could not hide it. But as if she had already prepared an answer, "Please discuss this matter with my father of confession." She told him his name and church. He served in a church in Shoubra[1].

Michael went to meet with him. The priest told him about her desire for monasticism from many years ago and her frequent visits to the monastery. He added that he blessed the decision, especially that the mothers in the monastery feel comforted towards her desire.

Michael was shocked. He went home, straight to his room. He closed his door and prayed while crying. He did not know what to do. He had made many plans and placed great hopes on that matter. Although he wanted to win her very much, he did not want to stand in the way of her sacred desire, lest he be blamed or judged.

He prayed a lot and he was really comforted in these prayers. He got an idea to go and talk to her father and hear his opinion. He found him sad and confused; he was not able to persuade his daughter to change her mind. He tried with different methods but failed.

Michael knew, from her father, that many had proposed to Marian earlier. She refused, saying that the time is not suitable yet.

Marian's father was happy when Michael offered to

---

help with that issue. Both of them tried again to convince her, but she was totally captive to the idea of monasticism. She was dreaming of the monastery and the monastic life in a way that expelled any idea about marriage or a family.

Time passed by and Marian decided that it is time to leave the world and go to the monastery. She chose a Sunday morning as her last day in the world.

Michael was affected with her decision. Whenever he was alone, he thought about her departure to the monastery, trying to find a reason why she would die to the world' as she told him once. He asked himself again, "Why does she have to leave the world now, when she is still young. She is a fresh rose just opened to the world. Why would she deprive herself of many pleasures?

What is there in a monastery that is better than marriage and all of the joyful things in the world? Couldn't she love Christ when she is married?" He was tired with all these thoughts.

He stopped eating and talking to others for days. He decided that he needed to visit her in the monastery. He did not want to influence her decision this time but to understand from her, why she acted like this.

In the monastery, he could not meet her. The Mother told him not to come again. She spoke to him about the salvation of his soul and how he should care about his eternity. She asked him to pray for Marian if he really loved her.

He never thought about marrying anyone else. He

asked everyone he met, priests and monks, about that matter. A monk advised him to spend a few days in a monastery. There, he spoke with the fathers about his problems and troubles. He was comforted a little. Few issues were clearer now. He slept well for the first time in a while.

A couple of months later, he returned to Al-Natron Valley. He loved them and they loved him. He visited them more frequently. He felt the fathers' love and their kindness. He also loved the monastic stories that they narrated to him or he read in the 'Paradise of the Fathers.'

The following March, during the Great Fast, he was able to take a week off from work and he spent it in the monastery. He considered that week to be the happiest time of his life. He prayed a lot and talked with many experienced fathers. The fathers felt that he was a blessed young man and a chosen instrument for the monastic life. He also felt a monastic baby growing inside him. This baby started growing with more readings and many trips to the monastery.

He stopped following Marian's news. He did not care much when he heard that her family had moved to a different city. He prayed, one time, that God may guard her and deliver her soul, preparing her for the Kingdom.

The thought of monasticism filled his life. It has become the bridge that he would cross to the eternal haven.

Finally he decided, together with the fathers in the monastery and his father of confession that he would join the monastery. He started his new life with joy and happiness. Whenever he remembered his story with Marian, he laughed inside. He thanked God who was leading him in His way of salvation. He thanked Him for her departure to the monastery. It was one of the reasons that led him to his current life. He totally forgot about her.

In his second year being a monk, while he was working in front of an oven, they told him that his family has come to visit him. When he finished what he was doing, he went to the guesthouse. He saw from far a man, his wife, and their young girl. He could not recognise them.

He was surprised to see it was Marian, her husband Sami and their child Margaret who was three years old.

She told him what happened, bravely and simply. She left the monastery in her second year. She discovered with the help of the mothers there that monasticism was not her way. She did not reveal everything to her father of confession before going to the monastery, and she was captive to the idea itself.

She thought it was not wise to spend her life in the monastery fruitless. It is better to live a normal life in the world and bring more fruit than living in the monastery by forcing herself.

One year passed since this visit. .

When she went to visit him a second time with her husband and daughter, Father Evlogious could not see them. It was the day when he wasn't to leave his cell.

She knew then that it was not appropriate to disturb him with her visits. She left him a small note with her name on it, asking him to remember her always in his prayers.

In his cell, Father Evlogious read the note, tore it silently and stood up to pray for them.

AT MIDNIGHT

At midnight, exactly at 12:35 am, the church bell rang, with sad tolls. Father Theophan rose from his sleep, groping in the darkness until he reached the door of his cell. He opened it and hurried outside. It was completely dark, but he managed to see the fathers coming from their cells to the bell tower. He joined them and walked with them in silence.

On their way, Father Tadros, the abbot, met them. He told them that father Theophan had departed!!

The fathers were sad and comforted each other, wishing that their deceased father would find peace.

Father Theophan wondered how could they say that he had passed away. He did not care though but continued walking with them until they reached his cell. All of them went in, where they found him stretched on his bed, covered with a brown cloth. Next to the bed, two monks sat with covered heads, one of them crying loudly.

The fathers, one after the other, kissed the father stretched out on the bed. Theophan was at the end of his line. He bent and kissed the dead father, then he could control himself no longer. He burst out laughing and said without looking at the monks, "I am not dead. I deceived you!"

No one heard him or answered him. Theophan was not annoyed, but followed them when they left for the church, leaving behind two of them to anoint the body.

The fathers sat on a long ledge beside the church, commenting on the news of his death. He heard them praising him and giving him holy qualities like those of saints. They also talked about his good conduct and they blessed him because he had reached eternity.

He found himself sharing with them in praising him, but from one side only. He felt a cool breeze blowing on his face. He put his hand into his pocket, and found that he had forgotten his handkerchief. He headed for his cell to bring it, but found the door was locked. He searched for the key in his pocket, but did not find it. He stood confused.

The bell rang again, wailing for the dead father. He forgot about the handkerchief and returned to the church, to find his brothers entering one after the other. He saw the coffin carried on their shoulders. He ran to take his place among them. He lowered his shoulder a little and felt the weight. He felt a kind of comfort throughout his body.

Inside the church they laid him on a table in front of the sanctuary. Some monks cried and he cried with them. The service began. He said to himself, "Thank God that He has given me a chance to repent. I could be in this coffin now, but God had pity on me and offered me another chance. I can consider this day my birthday. Thank you, God."

He then became aware of the monks moving towards the coffin, getting it into the sanctuary, and circling it three times reciting hymns accompanied by the cymbals. He could not share in the carrying of coffin because of overcrowding, so he thought of going ahead of them to the cemetery and waiting for them there until they arrived. There he found that some workers had finished digging a big hole near the door, and sat waiting with Father Lucas. He sat with them and was silent for a while. Then he asked the father, "Was he sick or did he die suddenly?"

He heard him answer, "He caught a fever in the morning and it did not take long. God called him and he responded, joyfully, perfect and upright. How lucky he is!"

Father Lucas saw tears in the workers' eyes. He rebuked them gently, "Be glad that he has gone to the everlasting paradise."

The procession drew near, with the bell tolling sadly. It arrived and the song of Golgotha was sung, sending awe into souls and over the place. Spontaneously, he sang with them, "The two pious men, Joseph and Nicodemus, came and took Jesus' body. They wrapped it in linen, put ointment on it and laid it in a tomb, praising...."

The song ended. The burial was over. The fathers who had buried him took the wooden coffin back. The abbot said the final prayer and gave a short sermon on the joy of being set free, and getting ready for that awesome day, in addition to praising the deceased father.

The fathers kissed one another and left. It was four in the morning. Father Theophan returned to his cell, got into bed, made the sign of the cross on himself and in all directions, and went to sleep.

In the morning, he found everything the same as it was before. Father Theophan went to his neighbor's cell. He was about to knock on the door when the monk came out. Theophan greeted him, "Peace to you, father". Then he asked him hesitantly if he had heard anything from his cell during the night. The monk answered that he hadn't; although that he had been awake till four a.m.

The monk then asked Father Theophan, "Why are you asking?"

"No reason."

"Did anything happen? Did you hear anything?"

"No, maybe it's something not important. If I am sure, I will tell you."

He tried to remember what happened and how. Was he dreaming? Did he see a revelation? Maybe it happened between wakefulness and sleep. He remained absent-minded and distracted, and spent most of that day pondering over what had happened. He made sure that none of the fathers had died. He went to the cemetery immediately and found everything as it was. He saw even the big dried bouquet of flowers that had been laid there by some family members of a monk who died earlier. It had a card with the words, 'You are now in Heaven, the place of the saints. Remember us, our father, before the throne of the Grace.'

Father Theophan sat in front of the cemetery, with his head in both hands, bent over, and began to think and contemplate.

'Suppose I was to really die tonight, where would I go? For so many years now I have been trying to get rid of the sin of judging and the sin of... What would they do with my cell? How would they distribute my belongings? Who would live in it? Perhaps it's Father... He has, more than once, expressed his admiration of its location. No doubt he would speak to the abbot and ask to occupy it as soon as the news of my death was announced, before others asked for it. How would my mother and younger brother receive this news? Would my death have a big impact on the monastery? Am I effective? Who would be assigned my work? Maybe it is Father ... He does this kind of work well. If I went to paradise, would I meet Father... and Father... who died before me?'

He looked at the cemetery again murmuring. "Maybe I would have been lying on an old blanket now, like those who went before me, with my arms crossed on my chest in the form of a cross, and a card containing my personal information. Anyone looking at it later would tell that I didn't complete seven years in the monastery."

He rose, walking with heavy steps, and went back to his cell. He surveyed every corner with his eyes.

Since that day, for sixteen years, the fathers got used to seeing Father Theophan stand before the cemetery, with his forehead against the wall, praying for a long time and holding a sheet of paper with the names of the late fathers, known in the previous and current generations. He laid the same paper before him on the altar to mention their names during the diptych.

During that period of time, he often kept silent, although friendly and gentle. He often brought palm leaves and wove them in a beautiful bouquet; adding some roses and then placing it in front of the cemetery. In the three occasions when the cemetery was opened to bury a departed father, he participated in the burial process, seizing the opportunity to see the place where his body would be laid, and recording its image in his mind.

Last year we went to that monastery to visit one of the fathers, who was a relative of ours. We found the fathers in a state of reverence, with the bell ringing sadly. When we inquired what the matter was, we learned that Father Theophan had departed the night before.

THE WAY

When Monica decided to take off the dress of the world and put on the wedding dress in the convent, her mother refused and wept and swore with every little and big thing in her life, not to let her do any of this as long as she is alive.

The last time when Monica and her mother were visiting the convent, Mother Athanasia[1], the mother superior, tried to calm her mother and to pave the way for her daughter to

---

1   Athanasia: from the name (Athanasius), meaning "eternal."

join the convent.

But her mother said, while her tears interfering her words: "No I will not let her leave us. I do not have anyone to take care of me after her father passed away except her. Do not ask me to live in my son's home, I hate to be a mother-in- law!"

Mother Athanasia patted her on her shoulder ensuring her that God is the one taking care of her, but she continued to weep and Monica wept with her too.

But God had arranged for someone to warn the mother from standing in the way of her daughter's salvation, and that she had to surrender to the will of God. Her father in confession, when he visited her, told her that God will not leave her, but in fact He cares of both her and her daughter.

Her mother, reluctantly, approved...

Monica rejoiced, the whole world could not contain her happiness. She joined the convent the very same week.

Her mother, in turn, moved to live with her son, taking part with them in the usual home tasks and caring for the young girl (two and half years) and the new born baby, while her son and his wife were at work.

Truly she was not totally content, but she got used to this life as time passed by. Though every now and then she remembered her daughter and wept, surrendering herself to anguish and weeping for hours, till God brought comfort to her heart.

And perhaps her continuous thinking of her daughter, and how she left the world with everyone in it and everything in it for her own salvation made her also think of her salvation. Hence, she started to pray and to read the Holy Bible, and even she learned the way to serve the poor of the church.

As for Monica, they accepted her happily in the convent, and they cut her hair (a symbol for death from the world). They gave it to her to keep in her cell as a reminder to her of the death of the body. It is known that the glory of the woman is her hair. It has the biggest share among her interests.

There she lived in obedience, loving tranquility, and loving her cell. Her mouth did not stop praying and praising during her work time in milking the cows, at sunrise and sunset.

She was not seen outside her cell, except in church services time and her work in the farm. She stopped seeing any visitors except the two times per year that her mother visits her with her brother, his wife and children.

In her cell, she started to memorize some of fathers' saying like St John Climacus and St Ephraim, the Syrian.

Nun Aribsima (Monica's new name) was counted as the most quiet and kind nun in the convent. Although she was known as a clever one in the principles of asceticism, she would humbly flee from any question asked by the other mothers in the convent, wanting to benefit from her virtues.

As the years passed, our blessed nun was going from glory to glory. When the war from devil was fierce, she would increase in the steadfastness, using the joyful name of our Lord Jesus Christ.

The mother superior wanted to care more for her, being new to this world. Aribsima did not allow her to treat her specially, as this may stumble the other mothers in the convent, especially the weak ones. She told herself, "There are more deserving mothers". She told the mother superior, "Your prayers are enough. I am sure that God will have mercy on me because of them."

But, in the sixth year of her nunnery, an earthquake shook her life. Someone came to the monastery with news that her brother and his wife had died in a bad car accident.

It was a shock for Aribsima. Overcome with the human nature, she cried that night as never before. All the mothers gathered around her, trying to comfort her with some biblical words and nice patristic sayings.

She was calmed down...

Of course, she did not leave the monastery to share in the funeral nor condolences. She was broken hearted, thinking sometimes about destiny of her brother and his wife and sometimes about his two children and her old mother who was by then over sixty years old. She comforted herself that God would manage their lives but could not figure out how He would do this.

She could not sleep that night, and the whole week she was full of all kinds of thoughts. Mother Athanasia came to her, telling her that they are visiting her mother to give her their condolences, on her behalf and the rest of the mothers. When the mother superior returned, she went to Aribsima's cell, telling her that everything is ok. The only problem that they face now is the two children (eight years and six years), who was going to take care of them now. "God will not leave them", this is what the mother told her.

After a few days, Aribsima's mother came to the convent with the two children. Aribsima ran to meet them, trying as much as she can to control herself. She was shocked to see her mother on a wheel chair; she was paralyzed as result of the horrible accident. Aribsima tried to hold herself again and welcomed them greatly. She, unusually, spent the whole day with them. The mother surprised everyone, challenging in a harsh tone, "One of two, either I leave the two children with you here and God takes care of me or Aribsima comes with me to raise them until they grow up."

Everyone was astonished...

Following a few seconds of silence, the mothers started to suggest alternatives. The mother superior said, "Do you have any relatives, can they take care of you?" She answered, "Not first degree. I cannot leave my grandchildren with strangers. Also, I do not want to be a burden on anyone."

A nun said, "Can they join an orphanage?" Hearing this, the mother cried out, beating her chest, "How can I abandon my flesh and blood to live in these places, hungry for kindness. Who can care for them more than us?"

A third nun said, "You know my mother that Aribsima is a nun now. It is not allowed for her to leave the convent and return to the world."

The mother used the bible, saying, "But God says, I desire mercy, and not sacrifice, why are you pushing me to talk more? How am I going to support the children and myself? Isn't it Monica's turn to take care of us as we did before?"

The mother superior said, "This is easy; the convent can send you your needs each month."

Aribsima could not endure more. She asked permission to leave and she went to her cell. There, she fell down on her face, in front of the icon of Christ and started to weep, praying.

"My kind God, I do not have anything to tell you now. You know my misery and what is happening to me because of my sins. Guide me to what I need to do. I am Your servant. I came out here, loving Your name, asking for Your mercy. You know I have no goal but You. If You want me to stay here, arrange for my mother. If not, I am your servant."

She stood up, washed her face and started reading in the Holy Bible.

As for her mother, the mothers convinced her to give them some time until they can think and figure out what to do. So, she left them, going home with the kids.

The convent had a saintly bishop who was full of the Spirit of God. He, unexpectedly, came to the convent that same week, saying, "I came today, driven by God, regarding sister Aribsima. They were surprised and bowed down to him saying, "This is what worries us now, we needed to hear the voice of God from you."

He looked at them and said, "I see, as God had mercy on me, that monasticism is not just walls nor rituals. It is an internal secret life. The nun needs a convent to incubate her struggle but it is not enough to be in a convent. I see myself, and you heard, about women living in the world the life of nuns, while other nuns living in convents, the life of the people of the world. We all learned that obedience is better than asceticism. Asceticism can lead to vainglory while obedience leads to humbleness. We know that humbleness saved many, with no effort.

I think you understand what I want to say. I see that Aribsima may leave the convent to take care of her mother and the two children. When God wills and she finishes her mission, she can come back, once more, to the convent."

The bishop stood up and prayed with them and left. On his way out, he took Mother Aribsima aside and comforted her until she is not sad any more on that subject.

Aribsima went home...

Her mother welcomed her, not believing herself. The kids, as well, were clinging to her neck, happily. Her mother started to apologise to Aribsima that she made her leave the convent that she loved and the life she chose. Aribsima answered bravely and happily that she was not sorry for that as long as that was God's will. She added that she was sure God will bless her because of this action. She then started to arrange the house and clean it, starting with the kids' room.

In the mornings she used to wake up early, praying the midnight prayer followed by the praises. When she finishes, it is time for the children to wake up for school. She washes their face, combs their hair and then prepares breakfast for them. While they are eating, she prepares their bags and escorts them to their school. On her way back, she buys what the house needs for food and other things. Once again at home, she prepares breakfast for her elder mother and feeds her, without eating with her. She fasted till three p.m. every day. Her mother left her and did not contest this.

When she finishes her morning routine, she enters her room, puts on the nun's clothing and starts praying. She then sits down reading in the Holy Bible and the lives of the fathers. After having her pleasure in prayers and reading, she puts off the nun's clothing and starts preparing lunch. If there are any clothes that need washing, she washes them until she brings the kids back from school. She arranges lunch for them. The evening, she sits with the kids for some time, helping them with their study.

And time passes by.... Aribsima considers the work she is doing at home as similar to the work she was doing in the convent. In the meantime, she finishes her whole daily canon with no reduction.

Aribsima did not share in any family celebration. She

locked herself at home the whole day except for the part when she buys the house needs and when she took her mother to the physician.

At home, her old friends used to visit her to ask about her and encourage her but she only stayed very little time with them, afraid to lose precious time and fleeing from non useful talks and from the sins of judging.

Truly she faced some troubles, many times, but the love inside her as a virgin to Christ was of great help to her against the attacks of the evil one.

From time to time, Mother Athanasia accompanied with some of the mothers used to visit her. They brought her some fruits, books and presents. Her happiness was great with these visits and these gifts. The mother comforted her, every time, that all the mothers in the convent are praying for her so that Christ will support her with His grace until she finishes her mission.

The girl and the boy grew up and their needs increased. Consequently, Aribsima's effort with them increased, especially when they brought her the school's and their friends' experiences. She was able to raise them in the Christian manner, using her patience and great love to Christ. It showed up on their words and action, inside and outside their home. She even took them, every now and then, to the convent to spend a day with her and the mothers.

Aribsima's home has changed into a convent from all the praises and prayer raised in it. The bishop used to come to her, to take her confession and encourage her.

Her mother passed away. One year later, a fine young man proposed to her niece. Aribsima was very happy and the convent helped her with the marriage expenses together with some savings of her mother.

The young man managed to find a good job with a big salary and his life settled down.

Now the way is paved for Aribsima to return to the convent. The bishop and the mother superior, together with some mothers, accompanied her, with great honor to the convent. There, they received her with a great reception, worthy of a blessed struggler. She came back victorious, and the devil missed his chance.

She is thirty-seven years. She was away from the convent for fifteen years. She was able to continue her normal life from her first day back in the convent. She even asked the mother superior to go back to her old work in milking the cows. The mother superior agreed, due to her begging.

Mother Aribsima lived until she was eighty, a symbol of kindness and sojourn. They said that she is the plant that gave more fruit than any one else.

She answered, practically, anyone who would claim that monks would not be able to live outside the monasteries and their monasticism is a necessity because they cannot live a normal life as the rest of the people and take up responsibilities.

The monk is a person with the ability to live in any place. He preferred the monastic life for many reasons that cannot be explained to those attached to the love of the world and its pleasures.